CURIOUS CARVINGS, ODD ODES & TALL TALES

OF THE ISLE OF WIGHT

CURIOUS CARVINGS, ODD ODES & TALL TALES

OF THE ISLE OF WIGHT

Unusual Stories - Well Worth Exploring

GLYN & DAN ROBERTS

Published by Brill Books 2012
ISBN 978 1 906 274 10 8

For comments or questions, please contact
curious.carvings@gmail.com

DESIGN & PRINT **Studio 6**, The Square, Wickham, Hampshire, PO17 5JN
www.studio-6.co.uk

With special thanks to Lindsey Maguire and Alistair Plumb for their hard work in designing and printing this book.

FRONT COVER *Sharp Island boy confronts tricky Portsmouth lawyer.*
PAGE 1 *Planning a practical joke on the Island's dimmest smuggler.*
PAGE 2 *Monks and Island bricklayers build a new abbey. But where?*
RIGHT *In remembrance of a true Gentleman of the Road.*

Contents

Invitation to a puzzle

Everyone enjoys a good story and the Isle of Wight has more than its fair share of them. Historic tales of smugglers, royal visitors, royal mistresses, ship-wrecks, lost treasure, French incursions... many of them are familiar and often turn up in local histories of the Island. However, this book tells other stories, equally good but less well known, equally local and often with a surprise ending.

Island residents and regular visitors may feel that they know the Wight inside-out and, while always enjoying its beauty, imagine that there is little now left to discover. Well, here's a challenge. Look through this book and see how many of the photos you recognise. Each carving and plaque was put up between 2000 and 2011 and all except one are in public spaces, quite visible to passers-by. Be they carvings, poems or stories, each one says something about the spot where it stands. Most are historically accurate, but one or two – "Knot Likely", for example – should be taken with a pinch of salt.

So, *you who know the Isle of Wight well*, how many do you recognise? Two? Three? If you can identify four or more, we're impressed! And you who are just visiting, would you like to find these curiosities during your trip?

As we've said, they are easy to see once you've narrowed down the search:

❂ Tales – These are actually not "tall" tales, but true stories of Island events and people, from the 11th century to the 20th. They appear on bronze plaques next to each carving.

❂ Carvings are usually stone plaques set into a wall. These are quite large, maybe 3 feet square. Glyn chiselled them, using basic hand tools, and each one has close local connections, often depicting an unusual person.

Bishop Odo tries to resist arrest
by William the Conqueror

✪ Poems are mostly bronze plaques fixed onto walls, though some are carved in stone. Hundreds of verses poured in after the Island 2000 Trust asked Dan to set up poetry boxes inviting people to write some lines. More came from a competition to write verses celebrating local bus stops, some of which have very odd names. For this book we have selected twelve poems, but there are many others – funny, serious, joyful or sad, often in unexpected places. Some poems we have printed in full, while from the others we have chosen a few colourful lines. Each is worth reading in full – and that means a visit.

But where are they? Eventually, you might come across all of them by chance, but this would take a long time. Quicker would be to work out their location from the poems and tales themselves. We give plenty of clues, though we've sometimes deleted a word or it would have been just too simple. (A good map of the Island would help with one or two of them.) And there is a third way to find them, easiest of all, which you can open at the end of the book.

Once you have worked out where they are, perhaps you will visit them. Who knows, a 'trail' might develop! Anyway, we hope you enjoy solving the puzzles and finding them as much as we enjoyed in creating them.

G.R. and D.R.
East Cowes

1 Shell-Fish Fisticuffs in 1852

One morning in 1852 a young boy, Freddie Attrill, was collecting shell-fish on the beach when another lad came along, told him to clear off, and kicked his bucket flying. Indignant, young Fred thumped the boy – only to be told by shocked attendants that he had just hit Albert Edward, Prince of Wales, and that he was now in deep, deep trouble.

The attendants hurried the Crown Prince back to his mother and Fred, too, went home, doubtless very afraid. After a day or two, he was summoned to the royal residence to receive his punishment. To his surprise, though, an attendant took him from room to room and finally into the presence of Queen Victoria herself.

To his even greater surprise, the Queen commended him on standing up for himself, and said that every Englishman had the right to earn a living, the beach was open to all and the Crown Prince had been completely in the wrong. She even gave Freddie two guineas to mark the occasion.

Many years later, to remind people of this event, Mr Attrill decorated his house with sea-shells and it became a well-known tourist attraction right up to the 1970s. Then the decorations began to deteriorate and most were removed. But one wall still displays a large sailing ship ploughing through the waves, all done in shells.

A clue: the sculpture is within 75 yards of the water.

2 A Ferry Silly Thing to Do

This poetry stone stands on a platform overlooking the river – but which?

KNOT LIKELY

The cars on board, the gates well shut, the ferry was to leave
*From ***** to make its crossing one chilly winter's eve*
But sat there quite immobile as the skipper called in pain
'What VERY THOUGHTLESS PERSON tied a reef knot in the chain?'

You wouldn't think it possible: each link weighed fifty pound
All welded up in solid steel and bolted to the ground
Yet somehow, as the ferry sat and waited in the rain
*Some Very Thoughtless Person tied a **reef knot** in the chain.*

It might have been a motorist who bore some sort of grudge
It might have been an admiral; it might have been a judge
But with what motivation? Can anyone explain
Why man or maid should want to braid a reef knot in the chain?

The skipper tore his hair out, he called the County Press
He radioed the Council to come and sort the mess
And they approached the Boy Scouts (as knots are their domain)
To see if they could puzzle out the reef knot in the chain.

A dozen Scouts pulled this way, a dozen Scouts pulled that
But still the chain stayed knotted up, they couldn't lay it flat
In fact by seven-thirty - and this is quite uncanny -
The very simple reef knot had turned into a granny.

So then they called the firemen who, when they came said, 'Please
Just stand aside and we'll soon have this knot undone with ease.'
They pushed and shoved till half-past ten, they couldn't work it loose
By when, the wretched granny knot had turned into a noose!

If you wait here for what can seem like half an hour or more
And watch that ferry motionless on yonder blessèd shore
Do not despair, but say a prayer - and hope it's not in vain -
That no Very Thoughtless Person tied a reef knot in the chain.

3 Monkey Business at the Bus Stop

****DOWN FARM
There are no apes at ****down Farm
It's such a shame
I'd love to hear that whooped alarm
Or see a gangling shadow flit or spot the
fresh banana skin
And wonder who was holding it.
There may be cows and sheep within,
But no apes live at ****down Farm.
It's such a shame.
(Anon.)

This is one of the poems that Dan installed next to a bus stop. Did you know that there are 750 pairs of bus stops on the Island, each with its own, unique name?

A clue: From this stop it's but a short ride to Calbourne.

4 William Arrests Bishop Odo

HIS GOLD SUNK IN THE MILLSTREAM

It is generally well known that King Charles I fled to the Isle of Wight before being taken to London for trial and execution. Imprisoned at *********** Castle, he tried to escape, but got stuck in the bars of his cell window. (Now that would make an odd carving!) However, not many people realise that another king, William the Conqueror, came to the Island, long before Charles, and had an almighty row here with his half-brother, Bishop Odo.

THE ODD TALE OF BISHOP ODO

After his victory at the Battle of Hastings, William the Conqueror made his half-brother - Odo, Bishop of Bayeux, and a trusted lieutenant - Earl of Kent. Some years later, William returned to France, naming Odo as Regent in his place and instructing him to rule wisely and well.

According to Ordericus Vitalis, a chronicler of the time, Odo behaved very badly, imposing new taxes, and robbing rich and poor alike. It seems he planned to use his new wealth to try to buy the Papacy in Rome. Having accumulated a

huge fortune, the Bishop and his men came to the Isle of Wight, meaning to sail to Normandy.

News reached William, however. He returned to England and confronted his half-brother at **********, charging him with betraying the stewardship in his greed for gold. He then ordered the knights present to arrest Odo. But Odo protested that nobody present could arrest him – not even William himself – as he was a bishop, answerable only to clerical law. And as for ill-gotten gold, he had none.

For a few seconds there was stalemate and the course of English history might have changed at that moment if the knights had backed Odo. But then the quick-thinking William stepped forward and arrested Odo himself, saying, 'Then I arrest you, not as a bishop, but as the Earl of Kent that I myself appointed!' Odo was banished to France.

But what of the treasure? William's soldiers searched high and low, until one night they spotted Odo's men going down to the millpond and pulling out, according to Ordericus Vitalis, 'sacks of wrought gold'.

Rumour has it that there still remains, deep in the mud, part of Bishop Odo's hidden fortune.

Doing some research for this sculpture in a book on medieval stone carving, I read that very few sculptors of the 11th century signed their work. In fact the author had found only one example. It said, 'Robertus Me Fecit' [Robert Made Me]. That seemed rather appropriate, so I added it to my modern "Gothic" carving. GR

5 A Giant's Footprint – Found in Green Shale (?)

The opening lines of this poem by Carolyn King read:

Somebody once told me that ***** had a giant
a fearsome fellow whose forays into the village
reduced the locals to tears (and reduced the locals!)
He lived on the cliff, but, not content with a diet
of birds and rabbits and fish, turned inland
to hunt for tastier morsels (and mortals)

Ancient tales of giants inhabiting the Island seemed to be borne out by the bones and blood-like rusty seepage that constantly emerged from the fossil-rich cliffs (with traces of iron) along the south-west coast of the Wight.

Here, Dan is bedding down the poetry plaque into its base on the Green, just one (giant) stride from a bus stop. But which?

6 Beware of the Bull

This lady is admiring another poem by Carolyn King, who has written and published many verses with Island themes. A powerful wooden carving of a bull by sculptor Paul Sivell inspired her to write some atmospheric and dramatic lines, which end ...

... on winter nights, when the sky is black
and storm clouds roll their thunder across the downs to the sea,
a sound like pounding hooves rings out across The Mall

And it's too dark to see if a huge black beast is tethered to a post.

THE BULL RING

I think it was the thunder of hooves that alarmed me most,

At first I thought it was my engine knocking
– driving at 20 through Brading High Street;
but suddenly there he was – this huge, magnificent bull.

Tethered now, he strains at the leash – a ring through his nose.
But when he arrived on that hazy September morning
I couldn't believe my eyes.

I wondered if this was really Hades in disguise,
abducting Persephone (via the Roman Villa),
his midnight-black coat steaming with white-hot rage.

the original tearaway – a mythological 'rocker'
He must have found it even harder than I
to keep to a steady 20 m.p.h. through the winding high-street.

No-one will ever know what really happened,
but it must have been something truly spectacular
– quite as amazing as watching St George slay the Dragon.

I dare say it took a dozen men to capture him, shackle him
to the stake and ensure he'd never be able to run amok again.
The village would never feel safe if it feared he might escape

Now he watches the traffic chugging sluggishly by
and the schoolchildren skipping along the road
where once he tossed his head and galloped so fierce and free

But on winter nights, when the sky is black
and storm-clouds roll their thunder across the downs to the sea,
a sound like pounding hooves rings out across The Mall,

And it's too dark to see if a huge, black beast is tethered to a post.

Carolyn King 2005

This poem was posted into the Brading Poetry Box

As a bonus to the poem and the sculpture (should you track them down) you will find set into the pavement the massive metal ring to which the unfortunate animals were tethered, years ago, to be set upon by savage dogs.

7 An Oblique Ode (at one of the loneliest bus stops on the Island)

Felicity Fair Thompson's poem praises this lonely down and claims it is unjustly named. These few lines offer a clue as to the bus stop's location:

> *.... and see not bleak but bountiful*
> *Not the dark overhang of Bagwich Lane*
> *But bright gold God-given gorse and*
> *blue sky. And at night,*
> *not interrupting town light,*
> *but stars.*

A clue: Beautiful in summer, yes, but few would fancy waiting for a bus there on a chill December evening, with the north wind howling across the down from Rookley.

8 The Monks' Centenary

In 1901, after a wave of anti-clericalism in France (following the notorious Dreyfus Affair, in which the French Army and some sections of the Catholic Church were involved) many thousands of monks, priests and nuns felt bound to leave for Spain, Italy and Germany. A hundred or so even came to the Isle of Wight.

At first, they found accommodation and built a small church at Appledurcombe, but then moved to another part of the Island, where an ancient monastery had once stood. Here, they built a fine new abbey, employing local bricklayers.

In 2001, the present Benedictine community asked Glyn to make a sculpture to celebrate the centenary of their arrival. He did so in triptych form (three panels). The first shows them hurrying away from their old abbey at Solesmes, bringing part of their huge library with them. The second shows the new abbey under construction, with architect-monk Dom Paul Bellot atop the scaffolding. The third shows the monks singing a

Gregorian chant, which has been a special feature of their community for many years.

This sculpture is made up of 52 interlocking tiles (terra cotta). Some, like the organ booming out a giant chord of music, are quite large and intricate. As damp clay tiles dry out, they shrink, and during firing they shrink further and quite often some will break. It would have been disastrous if any of this batch had shattered as we could never have made a replacement tile that would to shrink to fit. As it was, of the 52 tiles fired in the abbey kiln, not a single one broke.

The monks leave France taking as many ancient books as they can carry.

P.S. It might be worth taking a torch to see this sculpture as it is in a rather dark arched alcove of the church, though just 8 yards from the main door on your left hand side. Please respect any service that might be taking place.

Another puzzle: The sculptor signed his name in the clay before it was fired. The bold lettering is easy to read - once you've found it!

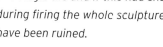

A monk at the organ. The instrument is one single tile and if this had shattered during firing the whole sculpture would have been ruined.

25

9 A West Wight Mystery

Early one morning, back in the 1840s, an old fellow was seen wandering the paths in West Wight peering curiously here and there. Presently he approached a man cutting willow twigs and hearing them called 'withies' gasped, 'My eyes! Withies? Why, that's what they calls 'em in the Isle o' Wight!' The farmhand retorted, 'So what? This is **********.'

At this, the wanderer seemed even more astonished. '**********?' he gasped, 'If there edden't a place with that very name over on the Island!'

At this, the farmhand dismissed him as mad and the old chap stumbled off, muttering, 'I can't make it out at all!' That morning he wandered as far as Wellow, perplexing folk he met by remarking that each place was 'terrbul much like the Isle o' Wight'.

At last the story emerged. Manny Young (for that was his name) had helped land smuggled brandy the night before at Totland Bay. Well liquored, he had fallen asleep in the boat. At dawn, a passing friend joked that during the night they had put to sea and were now over in France. Still groggy, Manny exclaimed, 'France? I han't bin in **France** afore! Now we're here, I'd like a bit of a walk, just to see the country.'

A clue: If you've done the long river walk from Yarmouth, pause at the Bier House and look around. (No, not the *beer* house – though there is one of those nearby, too.)

JOY

A chatter of children
way up on Tennyson Down
hurtling into space they had found,
excitement dispersing mottled gulls,
bowled along on skittled legs
        greeting the abundance of air.
Voices spiralling upward, kite-ward,
the day tilting them on
and beyond themselves.
        Wind heckling their burning ears
snatching at clothes
grasping at hair
fingers spread and webbed
with blue, feet paddling
        fast and faster,

swirls of laughter
scudding the sky,
        the joy of watching

children fly.

Eve Jackson 2006

10 Joy

· ·

Another bus stop poem, this time by Eve Jackson, who was delighted to see laughing children buffeted by the wind on Tennyson Down. We think the great poet himself would have enjoyed her lines, situated by an old drinking fountain a short walk from his house, nearly at the bay.

...Voices spiralling upward, kite-ward,
   the day tilting them on
   and beyond themselves
   Wind heckling their burning ears
   snatching at clothes
   grasping at hair.....

11 A Gentleman of the Road Meets the Queen

THEODORE RACINE SEARLE, 1916-1987

Very few tramps make their way to the Island, but one came in 1957 and stayed for 28 years. Theodore, known to most of his friends as Theo, was a tall, well built man, bearded, long-haired and wearing several layers of clothing topped by a duffel coat. He always wore rolled down Wellingtons. Well educated, nicely spoken and with good manners, he soon became a popular figure, although rather a mystery to many. All sorts of rumours abounded about him. He was thought to have been born of wealthy parents and paid to stay away from home. Some said a failed love affair blighted his life...

What we do know is that he was once a county and international trial hockey player. He was also a lover of music, played the piano and wrote

poetry. He lived close to nature and often slept in woodlands and barns. Theo spent hours watching birds and animals. He never begged and always behaved like the true gentle giant that he was: a threat to no one, a real Gentleman of the Road.

A few lines from one of his poems say it all about Theo:

By the old open oak I lie
Night after night, night after night.
A wayfarer as time goes by.

Derek Stirman, founder of the Isle of Wight Branch of Amnesty International, wrote the text above. Thousands of Islanders had seen Theo during the 28 years he roamed their woods and highways. Some steered clear of him, but Derek got to know him well. In 2006, he published a short book about Theo and thought of erecting a bench to his memory, but when Glyn suggested a carving, Derek jumped at the idea.

Carving and plaque were installed in a square of one of the bigger Island towns, right next to a superstore. They were unveiled by the Island's High Sheriff in the presence of the Town Mayor and councillors. The only other statue in the square is that of Queen Victoria. We think it's rather English and quirky to have monarch and tramp together sharing a public space.

A sobering thought that things don't change

When Glyn and Dan were tidying up after the unveiling ceremony, we discovered in the bushes behind the lamp post (see photo) the sleeping bag and cardboard bedding of a 21st century homeless person.

12 Miss Black's Bus Stop

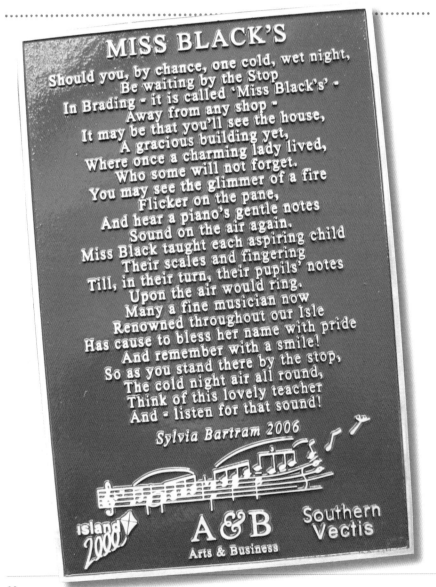

MISS BLACK'S

Should you, by chance, one cold, wet night,
Be waiting by the Stop
In Brading - it is called 'Miss Black's' -
Away from any shop -
It may be that you'll see the house,
A gracious building yet,
Where once a charming lady lived,
Who some will not forget.
You may see the glimmer of a fire
Flicker on the pane,
And hear a piano's gentle notes
Sound on the air again.
Miss Black taught each aspiring child
Their scales and fingering
Till, in their turn, their pupils' notes
Upon the air would ring.
Many a fine musician now
Renowned throughout our Isle
Has cause to bless her name with pride
And remember with a smile!
So as you stand there by the stop,
The cold night air all round,
Think of this lovely teacher
And - listen for that sound!

Sylvia Bartram 2006

island 2000

A&B
Arts & Business

Southern Vectis

How many knew why the bus stop called 'Miss Black's' was so named, until this poem by Sylvia Bartram appeared? And how nice to commemorate such an inspiring teacher of bygone years. But the story doesn't quite end there.

When we approached the people in the house by the bus stop to ask if we could fix a plaque to their garden wall, they welcomed it. However, a little later they phoned to say it would not be appropriate after all. We were quite disappointed, but then they explained their decision:

'Of course you may fix it to our wall, but ours is a modern house - not the building mentioned in the poem. Also, the bus stop has been moved since Miss Black's time, from her house to ours, a hundred yards along the road, but if you go up there, you'll see that hers remains 'A gracious building yet'. Lastly, one of her piano students still lives in the house to this day. If you ask her, she might let you have the poem on Miss Black's actual wall.'

And she did.

13 Oakfield

Who needs Regent Street or the Champs Elysées? It's great that Cléa Barton feels that her High Street has just about everything one could wish for.

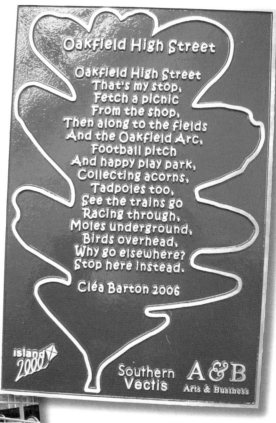

Oakfield High Street

Oakfield High Street
That's my stop,
Fetch a picnic
From the shop,
Then along to the fields
And the Oakfield Arc,
Football pitch
And happy play park,
Collecting acorns,
Tadpoles too,
See the trains go
Racing through,
Moles underground,
Birds overhead,
Why go elsewhere?
Stop here instead.

Cléa Barton 2006

island 2000

Southern Vectis   A&B Arts & Business

14 Furious Driving in East Cowes

In early January 1899, Mr. Henry House - inventor, manager of an East Cowes company making motor vehicles, and holder of UK Driving Licence No 2 - appeared before Newport Magistrates. He was charged with driving his motor wagonette at a speed greater than eight miles per hour to the public danger.

Police Constables Scott and Maber reported that they had compared watches at 10pm and set themselves to detect motor vehicles travelling at excessive speeds in the vicinity of East Cowes. P.C. Scott stood near Osborne Gates and his colleague waited at the bottom of York Avenue. The accused covered the distance in just three minutes – an average speed of more than 18 miles per hour.

The Chairman of the Board of Magistrates said that he understood how the public was terrified by motor cars driven at 'such a furious pace' and fined House £3, plus 11 shillings costs.

This was the very first motoring offence to be prosecuted on the Isle of Wight and led to a lively exchange of letters in the I.W. County Press. Some felt that House got his just desserts and that motor vehicles had no future on the Island. Henry replied emphatically that nothing could now stop the spread of cars, whether Islanders liked them or not.

Glyn writes: Carving this sculpture presented me with a few problems. First, I made a clay model, with Henry House looking like Mr. Toad ('Poop, Poop!') and driving an 1896 car, which seemed about the right era. I put my model on display at the East Cowes Heritage Centre, but it wasn't long before someone pointed out that the vehicle I'd chosen was completely wrong. 'House's motor wagonette was steam driven,' he said, 'a rather clumsy affair with a tall funnel. We have an old picture of one of his actual wagonettes, if you'd like to copy that.' A good job I hadn't gone ahead and carved the wrong type of car in Purbeck limestone!

Second, there was simply no suitable wall on York Avenue in which to insert a sculpture. We would have to build one, which is more easily said than done. It meant finding land on which to build and getting full planning permission from County Hall. This took over a year, despite the best efforts of East Cowes Town Council to move things along.

Thirdly, when I had almost finished carving the stone, I realised I had made yet another mistake, a glaring one and one impossible to rectify. All I could do was add a clue to the finished work to show that I knew of my blunder. The big day came for the unveiling and the High Sheriff of the

Island did the honours. I held my breath waiting for someone to say, 'Hey, that's surely wrong, isn't it?', but nobody breathed a word.

Should you visit the sculpture - it's easy to find - perhaps you will spot the mistake, with or without help from my Biblical pointer.

15 Duck Snub Outrage

'Down at the Quay
I saw a duck
And he saw me
I wished him luck

But not a word
Not a quack
Was to be heard
In answer back.
It is this lack...

...of common courtesy amongst apparently comfortable wildfowl, which
really should know better and have absolutely nothing to complain about
in their treatment at the hands of well-intentioned humans...
that makes me sad.
Ducks are bad.'

Anon.

Having installed 'Duck Snub Outrage', and guessing its author had a good
sense of humour, the following spoof letter was sent to him:

"Slipway"
Quayside
Duckville I.o.W.

Sir,

I write regarding the monstrosity which has been erected practically in the middle of my drive. Since it has been there, my family and I have been subject to all manner of abuse. Further, its installation has desecrated what is for us a holy site, blighting our lives.

Yours distraughtly,
D. Duck

How his reply got back we can't recall, but it read:

Dear Mr Duck,

I was much concerned, at first, to read of your distress, but have since taken time to visit the 'monstrosity' in question and must say that I now find your complaint laughable.

First, the poem itself is placed well above duck level and unless you and your kind have of late acquired the ability to hover, I cannot see how any of you has been able to read through the whole work. Merely glancing at it during a rapid descent to the water must, as I'm sure you would agree, leave one's appraisal of the poem flawed at best.

Concerning abuse, I can only assume that it has been levelled at you by swans as these birds certainly have the physical attributes necessary to study the work from a standing position.

As for the site of the plaque, not only did I observe no obeisance whatever from your family but rather a tendency to preferentially defecate on the very ground you claim as holy. In no religion of man or beast could this be considered acceptable in a place of reverence.

In closing, I would remind you that this poem is no mere doggerel. Our own researches lead us to believe it to be the missing fragment of The Bard's 14th Sonnet "All wette am I", described by Whitstable in his Tractatus of 1656 as "of a verie furious fowlness".

Yours respectfully,
Anon

16 Another Old Man of Binstead

The bird under the 'B' of Binstead is a Stone Chat.

Back in the 11th century the hamlet of Binstead ('the place where beans are grown') had several important royal quarries. The quality of its Bembridge limestone was such that it was shipped over the Solent to help build Winchester and Chichester Cathedrals and many other edifices on the mainland.

Later, the pits fell into disuse, but opened again in the 19th century when building stone was needed for the fine houses in newly fashionable Ryde.

After that, the Binstead quarries closed for ever, but they live on today in local street names (Stonepitts Lane, Pitts Lane). You can also see large bumps and hollows in the landscape between Binstead and the sea, especially along the little path that links Church Road with Quarr Road.

In 2003, builders digging foundations for new houses on Pitts Lane unearthed some large blocks of Binstead stone. An enterprising local councillor acquired some of these and erected them by the roadside. He then asked Glyn to carve a quarryman on one stone to remind Binstead residents of the historic importance of their village.

Later, the carving inspired some unusual road signs on the A3054 between Ryde and Newport.

To give away a trade secret: the Binstead stone was actually too soft to be worth carving, so I used a piece of Portland stone and fitted it into the bigger block. G.R.

There is in fact another carving, only a few hundred yards away, locally known as the Idol or the Old Man of Binstead and very much older than our sculpture. It is set above a gate to the Holy Cross churchyard and is possibly pre-Christian. However, recent research suggests that this ancient carving may actually portray a woman! So perhaps our quarryman can claim legitimately to be the 'Old Man' of Binstead after all.

17 SUPER store...

These three poems, short but poignant, are on an ancient wall right outside an up-market superstore.

'Boys: Grazed knees again? It's just as well skin mends itself or your knees would have been thrown out by now.'
Sue. 2006. Cowes Poetry Box

To read the others, you may need to visit the site.

18 ...and SUB marine

Dan was charmed by a little poem from Mr. L.V. Hall who, though getting on, still sailed his boat in Newtown Creek. Dan carved the lines onto a flat stone shaped like the Isle of Wight that he found on the beach not too far from where Mr. Hall kept his boat. (At some high tides, the verse appears through the water, giving it a magical touch.)

A few weeks later, Mr. Hall rang, quite delighted. 'I've seen the stone, he called, 'and it's wonderful. I've taken the family there and said that it's where I'd like my ashes to be scattered some day.' Then he added cheerfully, 'I can hardly wait!'

Happiness is...

A friendly tide and a wind that's free
When young white horses ride with me
If all the wonders of the world should flee
They'd never be missed when I'm at sea.

A clue: On entering the big field at Newtown, keep left.

19 A Tale From the County Court

Clue: The carts would have collided within a mile of this pub.

One day back in the 1860s, two pony traps collided on the Freshwater Road west of Carisbrooke. Seeking damages, the farmers involved took the case to the County Court in Newport.

The richer farmer had engaged a lawyer all the way from Portsmouth, but cunning though he was he could not undermine the poorer farmer's evidence. Then the farmer's young son was called, as he had also been in the cart. He looked a bit dim, a real country bumpkin, but his story closely matched that of his father. Perhaps a little too closely, thought the wily lawyer, and decided to cross examine the boy.

'*Tell me,*' he said, '*on your way to Court today, did you discuss this case with your father?*'

'Yus, Surr,' admitted the country lad.

'*And did he instruct you what to say?*'

'Yus, Surr. He done that, Surr.'

'Oh, he did, did he?' purred the lawyer, closing in for the kill, '*Then you must now tell this Court, word for word, what your father instructed you say.*'

'Well, Surr,' replied the boy, 'he said, "*Thomas, there'm a mighty smart lawyer coming over from Portsmouth today. And he'll ask you questions, and he'll try to catch you out. So there be only one thing you can do, nipper. You tell the truth, and no 'arm can come to you.*" ...and that's what Oi done, Surr. Bain't Oi right, Surr?'

And the poorer farmer won his case.

20 Millennium Stone

Having walked Hadrian's Wall in 1999, I was inspired by the sight of Roman inscriptions cut in stone 1,700 years ago. So for the new Millennium – with Climate Change and the frightening destruction of our environment in mind – I chiselled out a question for Islanders in the year 3,000 A.D.

'*Et in Arcadia Ego*' is an old inscription meaning 'I too (live) in Arcadia'. Arcadia was once the most beautiful, well-watered part of ancient Greece, scarcely recognisable as such today. One wonders how green the Isle of Wight will be in a thousand years and if anyone will still live here to appreciate it.

However, the sculpture is 20 feet up in a wall looking out over the Solent, with no public access to it at present – maybe in fifty years – so, really, it shouldn't have appeared in this book. G.R.

And finally...

We hope you have enjoyed this book – and if you know of other true, unusual stories about people or happenings on the Isle of Wight (hopefully with a curious angle to the tale) please let us know. We might be able to use them for future stone carvings and bronze plaques.

curious.carvings@gmail.com